FLOWING IN THE PROPHETIC

By Chelsea Kong

Just to say thanks for downloading my book, I would like to give you the audio book version 100% free.

Email: kayunkk@gmail.com

Printed in 2021-2022, Made in Toronto, Canada
ISBN: 978-1-990399-16-9
Legal Deposit, Library and Archives Canada

Dedicated to the Lord for His glory

I pray that this book will benefit all those who read it. I received my first prophetic word at a church end time meeting. I became more interested in the Bible. I was thirsty for the Lord and got baptised in the Holy Spirit and began to speak in tongues. I learned about intercession and how to hear the voice of God and spent 3 hours a day with the Lord. The gift of prophecy is one of the other spiritual gifts that the Lord trained me to operate in. I was still learning to develop a relationship with the Lord. Learning this gift is easy when you have this foundation.

Contents

Lesson 1: Definition of the Prophetic

What is the Prophetic? The definition is 1. accurately predicting what will happen in the future: "his warnings proved prophetic"
2. relating to or characteristic of a prophet or prophecy: "the prophetic books of the Old Testament"
The Bible is full of prophecies. We know that the Lord used the prophets in the Old Testament, but in the New Testament, He speaks to us through the Holy Spirit. It mentions the gift of prophecy, which believers are given by the Holy Spirit.

"For prophecy never had its origin in the human will, but prophets, though human, spoke from God as they were carried along by the Holy Spirit." (2 Peter 1:21)

The Bible also warns us that we have to test every prophetic word that is given to us by believers when they are led by the Holy Spirit to speak.

"But test them all; hold on to what is good, reject every kind of evil."
(1 Thessalonians 5:21-22)

In the future, there will be people telling you many things and claiming that they are speaking God's plan for your life, but you need to discern whether or not that is from the Lord. I have known people that said that the Lord gave them a scripture concerning my situation. God speaks to us directly and we should hear from Him first before anyone else. If a friend tells you that God gave them a word or their daughter about you and then they said God is testing you, you need to ask the Lord directly if this is from Him. Does it match the scripture and nature of God? People will claim that they heard from God, but may provoke you or deceive you. Then if you believe them, you will suffer the consequences if it's not from the Lord. People's concern isn't the same as God's will. We are accountable for our actions and the words that we speak. We are responsible when we didn't ask God for His counsel and confirmation. People will tell you that you don't have enough faith. Do they know what God's plan is for you? They are not God.

The Bible tells us we need to have at least two to three confirmations about a word that we receive. You will be faced with many voices telling you the same message and also others telling you something that seems contrary. Only in the stillness of His presence, you will recognize His voice and you must silence all others. The key to hearing actually from God is you must know the Bible to recognize His voice. There are three foundational points that we need to base the prophetic word on and know that each one has a certain measure of insight.

"But he that prophesieth speaketh unto men to edification, and exhortation, and comfort." (1 Corinthians 14:3)

"for no prophecy was ever made by an act of human will, but men moved by the Holy Spirit spoke from God." (2 Peter 1:21)

"For we know in part and we prophesy in part;" (1 Corinthians 13:9)

"do not despise prophetic utterances." (1 Thessalonians 5:20)

Prayer
Thank you for the Holy Spirit and the gifts even the gift of prophecy. Lord, I yield myself to you to be used for your glory. Fill me with your Holy Spirit. Baptize me. Activate the gifts of the Holy Spirit in my life. Cause me to become sensitive to the Holy Spirit. Use me for your glory. Lead me to those who need your ministry that needs to hear a word from the Lord for their situation. Open my mouth to speak your words to them and increase my faith to hear you. Cleanse me with the blood of Jesus. Anoint my lips to speak your words accurately in Jesus' name. Amen.

Practice Exercise
You can prophesy over yourself in a mirror or find somebody else to speak the prophetic word to. You can play instrumental music or worship songs. Pray using the gift of tongues and wait for the prophetic words to come.

Lesson 2: How to Hear and Receive

Keep this in mind whenever you receive a prophetic word from anyone. The person must be under authority and be tested as accurate. Many people can prophesy, but not everyone has the same spiritual insight. The accuracy may not be as much if the person is not anointed to prophesy. We need to follow the instruction of the Lord carefully and prayerfully. We should pray over the prophetic word and look at the scripture to find anything that confirms that it is from the Lord. The Lord will reveal more about what you need to do. You might have to put it aside. Somebody will confirm to you again if the word is from the Lord. Prophetic words are not meant to be a guide, but a confirmation of the Lord's direction. As we walk in faith according to the Holy Spirit and the Lord's instructions, we will see the prophetic words start to align with our life. It will then manifest. There is a time frame for every phrase that is given. We need to know the time frame. Some prophetic words take months or years before they happen. Some are very fast. It is advised to track the prophetic words. Keep a journal when it happens.

In Habakkuk 2, he teaches us how to receive from the Lord a word and a vision. We learn to wait to hear Him speak, see what He shows us, write it down, and speak it. Speak it by faith.

I will stand upon my watch, and set me upon the tower, and will watch to see what he will say unto me, and what I shall answer when I am reproved.

2 And the Lord answered me, and said, Write the vision, and make it plain upon tables, that he may run that readeth it.

3 For the vision is yet for an appointed time, but at the end, it shall speak, and not lie: though it tarry, wait for it; because it will surely come, it will not tarry.

My sheep hear my voice, and I know them, and they follow me.
(John 10:27)

So faith comes from hearing, and hearing through the word of Christ. (Romans 10:17)

This is the base foundation to hear God accurately and receive a vision from Him. This is easy to learn and apply to our lives. The Lord speaks in a flow. It will come to us naturally when we practice it daily. You yield yourself to the Holy Spirit. Our spiritual senses must be sharpened daily. You can pray to ask the Lord to sharpen your spiritual senses. You can smell and taste too. Some have smelt various fragrances. The Lord also can allow you to smell food that somebody is eating while you are on a virtual call. This happened when I was chatting with somebody on a video call. The person was able to smell and taste the pomegranate that I was eating. That is how connected you can become with somebody spiritually. The Lord is not limited to physical distance. You can be in two different parts of the world and still have a deep connection. Some have traveled to other places in the world by translation. God can transport His people spiritually without you having to leave the country you are in or He can translate you out of your body to another place. There is also supernatural transportation where He shortens the drive to your destination. This seems unrelated to the prophetic, but the prophetic is also about changing the future and the present situation. You can change a situation before it happens when the Lord reveals it to you.I also have a book and teaching guide about How to Hear God's Voice. You will be amazed because God can tell you a lot of details if you allow Him. It depends on your relationship with Him. It takes years to become strongly rooted in a deep relationship with Him.

Prayer
Father, thank you for the gift to hear your voice and discern it. Open my spiritual senses and cause me to become still in your presence. Clear my mind from every distraction, so that I can hear you. Thank you for your message in Jesus' name. Amen.

Practice Exercise
Start to practice listening to the Lord and doing what He tells you. You can write, draw, or record it. You need to become quiet and focus on the Lord. See yourself alone with Him. Believe that you heard Him. Then journal it. Check with the scriptures to see if this is from the Lord.

Lesson 3: Testing the prophetic word

"When a prophet speaks in the name of the Lord, if the thing does not come about or come true, that is the thing which the Lord has not spoken. The prophet has spoken it presumptuously; you shall not be afraid of him." (Deuteronomy 18:22)

"Beloved, do not believe every spirit, but test the spirits to see whether they are from God because many false prophets have gone out into the world." (1 John 4:1)

We will know based on these scriptures if the word comes from the Lord. We must be careful about nature in how the prophetic word is given. Some people may have pride when they speak. They will not want to explain or take responsibility for the word they have spoken. They will seek to protect themselves. They will tell you not to blame them if it doesn't happen or if they made a mistake. They may insist that you didn't follow the instructions given and that it is not that they gave the wrong word. They will tell you a specific time frame and question you about what happened and that you missed your opportunity. Be aware of those who ask for money. Some people tell you to give a certain amount and the Lord will bless you. You need to check with the Lord if He is telling you that. People will tell you this with various motives. You need to test the heart of the person also before you give it to them. It is better to give to the kingdom. You can give to a servant of the Lord, which the Bible calls the Terumah. It is a small tithe amount that is assigned to the servants of the Lord. There is a ministry called Eagle's Wings that discovered that the amount should be given and it is 2.5% of your income. You should ask the Lord if He wants you to tithe to the servant of the Lord and which one. It could also be multiple, but you need to be wise about this. Many people claim to be servants of God but are after money, power, or fame. You can test the ability to hear regarding this also.

There is one time that I gave to a pastor the Terumah even out of the small increase of income received, but eventually, I noticed her reaction.

There is an expectation that more is owed and required, so at that discretion discern and stop releasing when the spirit of mammon arises. Ask the Lord if there is a need to continue to release to anyone else. The fruit will show if the person is sincere and honest. There is another case where another pastor had insisted that one day I would release a large amount of offering to them. When one is truly serving the Lord, they will receive from the Lord from the right people and do not have to speak such things. The one who is the giver would be convicted by the Lord also. Otherwise, it is a false word. In another circumstance, a pastor believed that a business idea that she felt strongly about was the Lord's provision. When I found out more, I came to realize it was not the case because more money was required for it to work. Even with that, I realized the strategy in a sense. Greed is guaranteed to happen in network marketing businesses. There were a few of these and they always turned out to be a loss of money. If you believe that God told you to go into these kinds of businesses, you need to check with your spirit to discern if that is the Holy Spirit or the spirit of mammon. Greed will always advise you that you will make money from doing the business, but you will find that no success comes. Some people manage to gain profit, but it doesn't mean that they succeed to become rich, but they have taken advantage of others. They got paid out, but those who joined and didn't work or couldn't get it to work out for them had no financial benefit. The system may seem good, but once tested it is a failure for them. Even a vision can be deceiving when it comes to focusing on money.

Jesus Christ warned us that the rich cannot enter into the kingdom of heaven easily because of their love for money and possessions. He did not say that they can't be saved. He only said how hard it is for them. Many of the patriarchs became rich and even the apostles have possessions of their own more than an average income. Luke is a doctor. Matthew is a tax collector. Peter and James owned the fishing company. They all had some kind of business or profession that was successful. The word tests our heart also. The words that come from our heart reflects our nature. Sincerity and honesty of character bring the accuracy of the prophetic too. My co-warrior in the Lord, Gracious Dcruz, said on March 23, 2022, "Great fear of God and a sense of justice (conscience) is the balance that weighs between right and wrong." The fear of the Lord is what keeps us walking uprightly before the Lord at all times. When you ask the Holy Spirit and check your heart is right before Him, then you will know that the words you speak are accurate. There will be a confirmation and conviction. If there is somebody with you that you are speaking the prophetic words to, they will verify that it is from the Lord. There will be a great joy, peace, and liberty. It will bring comfort, edification, and exhortation to them. It will be aligned to the scriptures and God's character. Other people will know that it is from the Lord because their spirit will convict them. This will protect you from deceivers. They can be sly in hiding their character or can be very obvious. They will be out of protocol and their spiritual foundation is not correct. Some are self-appointed and spend all their time in prayer but they don't go out to minister and share the gospel with others.

Character is important as a prophetic presbyter, minister, or prophet. You need to have the character of Christ and the fruit of the spirit. There is a sister in Christ that often speaks negatively about others and when she tends to be accurate when asked questions and she is not even praying when she speaks it. The attitude however is not in line with God's character even if the word is correct. An approved prophetic voice and prophet has been proven and recognized by others in leadership. A prophet must follow the protocol of the church leadership before they can speak a prophet's word. When laying hands, that person also must follow protocol and be tested and approved as prophetic. You can reject the word from them when you discern their character or spiritual foundation is not in line with the word of God. The gift of prophecy is also Jesus Christ. Be careful of wolves in sheep's clothing. These ones act like they know the word of God but when confronted with the wrong doctrines they are in denial. We are warned not to share in their destiny and judgment.

I know a pastor that has tested the prophetic words and counsel the Lord has given through me and confirmed that they are accurate as he applied them and it worked out. The results were the same as the Lord revealed.

There are various examples of prophets giving a word to Israel. Elijah

told a widow to gather as many empty vessels from her neighbors as pos
sible. She was to close her doors and pour the oil from her small cruse
jar into each empty vessel. Only when there were no more empty ves-
selsto use, then the miracle stopped. There were many jars filled with
one small cruse of oil. He told her to go and sell the jars of oil that she
filled to pay off the debt that her husband owed and to live off the rest
of the money. The Lord will provide you with more than what you need
to give to others. God's nature is always out of compassion and love for
others. There must be 2-3 confirmations to prove the word is from the
Lord. Each phrase has a different timing. Each word must be declared in
faith until it is fulfilled as you follow God's instructions daily.

Jesus also gave thanks to the Father for over five loaves and two fish that
a boy contributed for 5000 men to eat along with their families. When
Jesus told the disciples to pass the basket out, then the food multiplied
and after all, had eaten there were 12 baskets full.

Prayer
Father, I pray for your Holy Spirit to give me discernment to recognize
which prophetic words are from you and which aren't. I pray that the
words that I speak will be accurate and from you. Inspire and increase
the anointing on my life to speak accurately and that the fear of the Lord
rises within me. Keep me humble and righteous. Protect my heart from
evil and that people will know that the Lord is speaking through me in
Jesus' name. Amen.

Practice Exercise
Find a time to sit to be alone with the Lord. Spend time to worship,
praise, thank, repent and seek Him. Read the Bible and then wait for the
Lord to speak. Write, draw, or record what He gives you. You should
practice this daily and study His character from the Bible. Learn also to
take time to rest in His presence. It will sharpen your spiritual senses and
develop your relationship with Him. You will begin to hear His voice
more clearly and accurately. Then you will recognize Him.

Lesson 4: Operation of the Prophetic

Most people who prophesy are baptized in the Holy Spirit and speak in tongues. The gift of tongues will charge the prophetic gift to flow. Faith is necessary to prophesy. You must be able to believe God for what He wants to say and wait upon Him to receive and then release it to the receiver. This also works when you want to receive dreams and visions for what you are asking God to show you. He can give you dreams, but if you have a specific request you must believe He will answer and show you. The closer you are to the Lord and the more time you spend with Him the greater the flow. Some prophetic ministers require worship music or a minstrel to play for them before the prophetic word flows. In an atmosphere that is rich with God's presence, this gift can flow. Tehillah's high praises also can stir up the gift to operate. Everyone in Christ can prophesy when the Holy Spirit touches them. The Holy Spirit should be free to operate wherever you minister. Jesus went to those the Lord led Him that were open to receive Him. It is possible to give a negative prophetic word if we are not careful. Elisha spoke a curse over some boys that made fun of him for being bald. We are responsible for the words we speak. Make sure your conscience is clean before God. When the anointing comes, we need to release the word.

"Since we have gifts that differ according to the grace given to us, each of us is to exercise them accordingly: if prophecy, according to the proportion of his faith;" (Romans 12:6)

"If I have the gift of prophecy, and know all mysteries and all knowledge; and if I have all faith, to remove mountains, but do not have love, I am nothing." (1 Corinthians 13:2)

I was given a word before that I was seen wearing this cherry blossom-style pink Chinese winter vest. I was told twice that I have this, but I didn't physically have it at that time. It was years later that I visited the Pacific Mall and the pastor I was with at the time and I were looking at the Chinese winter vests and only one store had the exact pattern that she saw. It fit me and I bought it, so this fulfilled the word she said and it was a vision too. There were other prophetic words also.

The Lord has given me ideas for designs, writing books, business names, numbers, dates, places, ministry ideas, and songs. He also has given revelation, declarations, and many other insights. Whatever He gives you will bring you success when it's done correctly. He will guide you on when to release and how to succeed. He can show you or give you details. The Lord reveals precise times and tell about the people you will meet. The Lord tell you which person to pray for and what will happen in the future. One time the Lord disclosed that my cousin was dating. I found out she was but it was only for a short time.

There is one minister that she a widescreen view as a vision. He can receive all the details of the person's life and what is to come up to the time the Lord wants him to see.

Habakkuk received visions and was told to write them down and to hold onto them until they happen. Whatever the Lord reveals to you, we must learn to declare the prophetic words with full faith. It is better to maintain having time alone with the Lord in prayer, praying also in the Holy Spirit, reading and declaring the scriptures, worshipping, soaking, and hearing His voice.

Recently, I joined a church with somebody that I used to live with and during the prayer meeting, the pastor asked me to pray. The Holy Spirit gave me the words to pray and it covered all aspects that need to be prayed over. This is a prophetic intercession prayer, but also apostolic.

The prayer was inclusive of from the perspective of the seven mountains, which are also the kingdom spheres of influence on the earth. Not many people pray this way. I recall it was Monday, November 15, 2021, when I prayed that prayer. A member in the Miracle Time Zoom prayer group spoke to me months back on May 30th. I connected with them. We chatted on and off over the months until July 30th. That same day, a friend told me that I need to commit to spending time with the Lord again while I am not working. I decided to commit that the next day I would spend time with the Lord.

I was seeking the Lord and enjoying His presence. I sent a message on November 16th regarding my books to one of the group members on Miracle time. The next day, I received a message on my phone through Whatsapp asking me to pray for the person. They also asked me to connect through Telegram. The Lord is gracious and compassionate towards my situation. He sent me Gracious to help me in a time of need through prayer to overcome obstacles in life. He later brings in a John like the Revelator and he also receives revelations from the Lord. The Lord sent a Jew during the time of Purim to speak and confirm my heart motives and prophesy into my future when your life is going on track and improved yet on the journey to greater success. When you fast and pray, the revelations become more accurate, and more is revealed to you. The Lord will also bring the answers that you need. The timing is so perfect for your needs. The Lord knows who is for Him and rewards accordingly. As you operate, you must know your authority in the Lord also. This will be discussed in a later lesson in more detail.

When you are praying with a prayer partner, you will also increase in the gift and other gifts will be activated especially if you fast and pray. The Lord can cause you to become active in a few gifts that you haven't ex perienced before. I discovered the interpretation of tongues later on. The Lord caused me to operate in the word of knowledge on a deeper level in sensing the root of sickness or weakness. The person confirmed having a headache at the exact spot the Holy Spirit revealed. The Lord also said was the root cause is and then He reveals how to deal with it. Twice I experienced the ability to smell in the spirit. This is not an example of the prophetic but sometimes the Lord reveals that somebody will have an accident or get sick. I also received visions related to this and word of knowledge.

Prayer
Father, teach how to operate in the prophetic every day. Cause me to become sensitive to the Holy Spirit and to yield to you to allow you to use the gifts that you desire for each person as needed. Keep me in your presence every day and minute. Increase my awareness of you and the supernatural in Jesus' name. Amen

Practice Exercise
Take time every day to pray by the Holy Spirit. Use this gift of tongues to speed your spirit man and enable you to receive from the Lord. He will speak to you and you will be able to operate in the gifts of the Holy Spirit. The gift of prophecy may require you to listen to music to activate it also. Some people need this, but not everyone does. It will make the flow easier. Release the word that comes. You may get a vision, trance, scripture, etc. You may have to operate by faith that you received the word and speak it out. Try to record the word, so that you can listen to it again or remember it and pray over it. You can practice on yourself daily to increase the gift.

Lesson 5: Prophetic Words

I was unaware of what would happen next. The following day, November 17th I was asked to call. We started to spend time chatting and praying. The Lord began to reveal strategies and incidents that I needed to know. After that, the Lord used this chat and prayer time to train me for ministry. I began to flow in seeing visions and strengthened in the prophetic, but also spent time praying in tongues, worshipping, and waiting on the Lord. I enjoy dancing every so often, but usually on Sundays during worship time. As you serve the Lord, the gift grows. The more you use it to prophesy over people, the more it grows especially if you do it daily. The word of wisdom and word of knowledge will bring revelation into the situation.

On November 19th, the Lord gave me a prophetic word for a friend. She was so touched listening to it that she also wrote it out on November 22nd and asked me to review it. Then she posted it on her page but hid my name so that nobody knows who spoke it. Somebody commented and confirmed that the word is accurate. The Lord also told me that the prophetic gift He gave me is very accurate.

On December 9th, I got a call from a friend that was my colleague at a previous job. The anointing was so strong that I began to prophesy over her. She was thankful after receiving the word of the Lord.

The Lord will reveal to you things about others that you don't know about. That is how they know it is God speaking through you. I had this happen several times when I was ministering to people in a previous church. I also felt God's presence as I was praying for the person. People verified that the Lord's presence is very strong when I pray. There was a sister who even shook because the presence of God was so strong. The Lord has also given a strong healing anointing. It is the Holy Spirit that has the gifts. We are the carriers and the vessels, which allow Him to release it. If we are willing and obedient and walk in His nature and by faith, we can flow naturally. The more time we spend alone with Him even to rest in His presence enjoying Him will increase the anointing and allow it to flow. I spent many hours in the first few years seeking, resting, soaking, reading the Word, praying in the spirit, singing in the spirit, worshipping, and praising Him. I also enjoyed dancing before Him. That created a deep intimate relationship with the Holy Spirit. Holy Spirit is the singing spirit. He loves it when we sing with Him.

I have heard God's audible voice at least twice, but not a loud voice like others. It is important to know how to hear God when you operate in the prophetic. I have a book called "How to Hear God's Voice" that teaches children how to do this. It explains the different ways God speaks to us. He has spoken to me in most of them. When I started, I began to hear Him. I got scriptures, thoughts, feelings, and the still small voice. I often have dreams. I began to see visions years later, but I still, want this gift enhanced. The Lord will bring people into your life to equip you. If you want to grow in the gift of the prophetic, you need a mentor that is operating in the gift. Some people are called to be prophets and the Lord will confirm if you are called to be a prophet. It takes years of training and the Lord will isolate you. It can be a painful process. He needs to prune your character.

The Bible tells us the following regarding prophetic words:

And it shall come to pass afterward, that I will pour out my spirit upon all flesh; and your sons and your daughters shall prophesy, your old men shall dream dreams, your young men shall see visions: (Joel 2:28-32)

 But there were false prophets also among the people, even as there shall be false teachers among you, who privily shall bring in damnable heresies, even denying the Lord that bought them, and bring upon themselves swift destruction. (2 Peter 2:1-22)

We must have confirmation when we give a prophetic word or receive from others that are aligned with the scriptures and character of God. Holy Spirit can give you prophetic words through the speaking of tongues. He may touch your spirit to sing prophetic songs. I like to keep a recorder and use it in case He does. Prophecy can also change your prayer life. I found my prayer life became more prophetic, specific, strategic, and broad as it covered all areas of concern. It was not just personal but also related to the church, local, national, government issues, and global. The global is usually focused on revival. The Lord is concerned about families, youth, and children too. He amazed me whenever I prayed with others. The more anointing and time that I spent with the Lord the more amazing the prayers are. Worship has a powerful impact also on the prayers and soaking will let you yield more to the Holy Spirit. He will give you accurate details.

An example if you are in a court case, the Lord can give you the list of objections, instructions on what to do before and at the court hearing, and what to do after the case has been closed and you won. He will tell you the time to do something. He will reveal the attitudes and motives of the people's hearts and the verdict and judgments. He will also tell you the set of instructions on how to manage the finances after the case is won. He will reveal what happens to the opposing party and details about them. He can tell you the plans of the enemy and the solutions.

Prayer
Father, thank you for the gift of prophecy. Thank you for your guidance in every situation. Let me flow in your anointing to release a prophetic word to others. I want to be a pure channel of blessing for your glory. That those who meet me will be blessed. That only words of encouragement, comfort, and exhortation will be given with solutions. Lead my steps to those who need to receive a word of prophecy to change their lives in Jesus' name. Amen.

Practice Exercise
Make time to receive revelation from the Lord. Focus on a specific situation to pray into and allow the Lord to address that matter. He will reveal the matter to you and the solution. Speak what the Lord reveals and speak into the situation. Your prayer in tongues will change the outcome of the enemy's plans to turn against itself and bring victory. Visualize with your spiritual senses what the Lord wants you to see. The Lord can also tell you more.

Lesson 6: Visions

I found that I was receiving visions when I asked the Lord specific requests. He showed exactly what I needed to see. There was a day that I was praying for my father's breakthrough. The Lord gave me a picture that he is wearing a golden crown on his head. The interpretation that was explained is that he will receive salvation, so I was instructed that same night that I should call him to speak to him and lead him to receive Christ. I followed and it happened that my father and I spoke over a video call. I shared with him about my relationship with the Lord and then led him to receive Christ. The following day I prayed for my mother's salvation. The Lord again showed a vision. She was shown wearing a crown on her head also. I knew that it meant salvation, so I made the call to speak to her and lead her. The next time I prayed for my sister and again received a vision. This one showed her looking at Jesus while she was in a pasture. She went to Him. She saw Jesus on the cross. The Lord revealed she will be saved too. I had to trust Him for the words to speak.

The Lord also revealed a vision during worship service. I saw the glory of God was poured down upon the roof down to the foundation of my family's home. I knew the Lord is going to transform all those in that house. They will all know Him. He also instructed me about baptism. Growing up, the church I attended didn't practice water immersion baptism. The real baptism is water immersion and not water sprinkling.

Abraham was acknowledged as having a powerful ability to see prophetically into the future. He saw Jesus' death on the cross. That is many years into the future. Joseph prophesied also about the Israelites would take his bones with them out of Egypt. Moses knew that he would deliver Israel from Egypt. Moses was given the design for the Tabernacle. Aholiab and Bezaleel were given the gifts to create the designs. Elijah and Elisha have known prophets. Elijah also had a visitation since the Lord took him in a chair of fire. Samuel is known as a seer in the Bible. King David was anointed with the power of the Holy Spirit. He spoke wrote some songs that are considered prophetic. David also must have seen or known what was required to build the temple of the Lord.

His insight is powerful. The design for the Temple was made too. Many others in the Bible have a prophetic insight to see into the future. Ezekiel received visions from the Lord. Anna the prophetess knew from the Lord about Jesus being the Savior of the world. John also saw visions and recorded the Book of Revelation. Paul saw a vision of a man in Macedonia who wanted him to come and help him. These are only some of the more known individuals in the Bible. Jesus is the spirit of prophecy. He always speaks prophetically.

God can also show you visions of the future of His kingdom and anything else He wants you to know. He also wants you to share with others for a purpose. The seer's anointing is still in operation. The Lord still anoints individuals with the ability to see into the future. There are examples in the Bible of those who have visions, prophetic insights, or they are a seer. The Lord can show you visions concerning His plans for your life. He will tell you what He wants you to do and will direct your steps. It takes sometimes years to see the vision happen.

An example that I received from the Lord was a vision that the believer was under the ground. There was a hole above his head and the sunshine was shining down from above. Above the ground, plants are growing. It is a field of ground. The growth is coming from under the ground, but people didn't see it until it came forth out of the ground. The glory of God and victory have been promised as well as abundance and prosperity. A life that has been depleted and reduced to become small and seems lifeless will one-day experience greatness again. The Lord Jesus Christ died and was resurrected and this person also will be from their situation. They will be taken out of the pit that the enemy dug for him. The Lord will raise him again. New life happens and the roots are strong. The person will bear much more fruit in their latter days than their former days. Their life is like Job. They will become more blessed than before. This is a summary and some aspects of the prophetic word that was given. The Lord's grace is sufficient for His people. When we are faithful, the Lord rewards us. Our life will overflow. The Lord will judge and deal away with our enemies. He will restore to us 7x what we lost and gives us double for our trouble.

If you have the seer's anointing, you will have visions regularly and the Lord will give you personal visions to guide your life. You need to write down the visions that you receive from the Lord. If you have the same vision twice then it is a guarantee that it will happen though you may not know the timing for it believe that it will happen. God can make it happen to you. You just need to follow the leading of the Holy Spirit and focus on what He tells you to do each day. He can do something supernatural related to heaven or on earth. There is a time I went to a store and found a blouse and another time it was a jacket that my pastor saw me wear in a vision. I just went out expecting to find the jacket knowing that I will have it. The blouse was unexpected as I was going for a shopping appointment at La Chateau Outlet store and it happened that the blouse was there and it was the only one of its kind and fit me. I didn't have to pay for the clothes that I collected that day because it was a bonus for those in need going for employment. It was part of a program that I had enrolled in that led to the connection to an organization that helps those in need with employment attire, accessories, and items.

Another example of a vision is the Lord showed me the throne room. He is seated on the throne and I saw the crystal glass floor. Beneath it, the galaxy was shown and the earth was large in size and bright lights were shining all around it which are the believers and I believe they are the ones filled with the Holy Spirit. There is also a man kneeling in the prayer which is my prayer partner and the Lord Jesus called me "Daughter, come and pray with us." He knelt down near my prayer partner and put on the prayer shawl to cover His head and I put down my flags and went over to kneel down and cover with a prayer shawl too. This same room has television screens all around it in a circular layout and it has different pictures on them. Father God is watching everything that is going on the earth from those screens. I have seen this at least twice.

The Lord has allowed many other visions also to be shown including those more personal about life events. There was one time regarding the job. The Lord showed me the time that I worked in payroll and then at one office that I used to work at. He also showed me the one manager's office and and there is a volcano sitting on top of the desk. This is how the Lord led me to go back and study again and pursue a career in payroll. He will equip you to become successful when He leads you. You just need to follow the steps that the Lord reveals.

The visions can play out like a movie. There are visions that the Lord gave that were like this. The Lord showed from one scene to the next to the next about what will happen. There is always favour for God's people who follow Him. The wicked are dealt with according to His righteous judgement. The warfare is always first in the spirit realm before it is manifested on the earth.

An example for somebody in a court case, the Lord can reveal the courtroom and show how the court case proceeds and what is the end result. Jesus is our Advocate and intercedes on our behalf. God is the judge that demands on Satan for what he has stolen and done. In the earth setting, the judge enters the room and calls order in the court. The accused has an advocate that speaks to represent them against the offender or petitioner. The other individuals that are involved with the petitioner will also be judged for their part. He will give the closing verdict to the case. When the accusations are false, the Lord will reveal victory for the accused but a sentence to prison for the petitioner. Then the accused is signing off to close the case and gain back what belongs to them. The Lord will show the restoration. He can show the petitioner and their participants being arrested and granted an opportunity to gather whatever they require if necessary. You may see police involved in the arrest. The Lord may show you what happens after the arrest.

He has shown about future churches, ministries, and businesses that He wants established on the earth. He will provide and may show you how He will accomplish this. The Lord will also limit what we receive from Him. He does this to keep us walking with Him and to believe and trust Him. If we know everything, we may not experience the tests and training He has for us.

About the ninth hour of the day he saw clearly in a vision an angel of God come in and say to him, "Cornelius." (Acts 10:3)

And a vision appeared to Paul in the night: a man of Macedonia was standing there, urging him and saying, "Come over to Macedonia and help us." (Acts 16:9)

Daniel had many visions during his captivity in Babylon. He had the interpretation of them too. There are visions that haven't been fulfilled yet. The fall of Babylon, the reign of Medes and Persia, and others. We are in the time of the ten toes kingdom prophecy to be fulfilled. The UN has been going through this process of adding and subtracting earthly kingdoms. Israel will not be part of that. We are aware of the nations that are rising against Israel prophesied in Ezekiel and other books of the Bible. He is an accurate prophet. In Daniel 10:4-6, the Lord gave him eyes to see a vision that scared him. He was by the great river of Hiddekel. He met "a man clothed in linen, whose loins were girded with fine gold of Uphaz: His body also was like the beryl, and his face as the appearance of lightning, and his eyes as lamps of fire, and his arms and his feet like in colour to polished brass, and the voice of his words like the voice of a multitude." It said in verse 8, that Daniel was the only one that saw the vision. The other men that were with him experienced a great quaking on them and they hid.

Prayer
Father, open my spiritual eyes to see into the spiritual realm what you are doing. Cleanse my spiritual sight and forgive me anything that I have seen that dishonors you. Restore my sight. Anoint my eyes to see visions. Equip me and anoint me. Let me see everything that you want me to see. Cause me to see clearly. I desire the seer's anointing to receive from you in Jesus' name. Amen.

Practice Exercise
Visualize Jesus and let Him take you further into the vision. You may see an image in your mind. The Lord may allow you to see a vision immediately. Focus on the vision that He gives you to pay attention to the details in it. Try to keep a record of what you see. It is important and the key that you need. You will need to also pray over it and apply what you see into your life.

Lesson 7: Revelation/Word of Knowledge

Praying in tongues is also a requirement when you want to receive from the Lord a prophetic word. Elisha replied on a minstrel to stir the anointing so that he could prophesy. Worship is very important too. I found that when I thank, praise, repent, worship, and pray in tongues the prophetic flowed a lot easier and quicker. It is strong that I have to release all that the Lord wants me to speak before I can stop speaking. That is the flow of the anointing.

There was one time a sister came to church and when I prayed for the Lord revealed that she needs to use her real name and not the name that she was told to use. I asked her about her real name. She said that the name she is using now was given to her by her mother-in-law. I told her that she must use her real name because she is being capped by the other name. People don't realize that names impact people's lives. The prophetic can operate with the word of wisdom and word of knowledge. It is a revelation from the Lord. God will provide the strategy that the person needs.

The word of knowledge reveals what a person has already experienced whether that is the past or the present. The Lord will tell you exact details or some details about the situation. People's names may be revealed. Then the Lord will require you to deal with it. You should not delay. Some incidents may have severe consequences. God can tell you what somebody else is doing behind your back when you are unaware. He can tell you what they are saying too. The Lord will reveal mysteries to you.

A word of prophecy came that revealed the current situation in detail. The Lord revealed the mind of people that are involved in the situation that a believer is dealing with. He revealed also the situation that the person is faced with and what is the reason for the current situation. I have noticed that women these days are not always faithful to their partners. They will go to the pastor seeking counsel and healing, but they don't want to be with their husband or take on their responsibilities. They find ways to escape and even some of them lie to the pastor and hide that their husband called them. They seek to please the pastor rather than the husband. They spend their time with the pastor to avoid going home Some individuals were never true believers but married to those who are and became snare. Sometimes even believers make the mistake to marry the wrong person and suffer from it. The Lord revealed in one case that a woman never committed her life to the Lord. She had taken away finances and enjoyed a good life, but made her spouse suffer greatly and mocked God. She did everything possible to come against her spouse, which is the Lord's servant. She did not fear the Lord. The Lord showed a vision that she will even fall into hell and her children also.

For to one is given by the Spirit the word of wisdom; to another the word of knowledge by the same Spirit; (1 Corinthians 12:8)

Prayer
Holy Spirit, activate the word of knowledge in my life. That other will know that you are an all-knowing God. You know the past, present, and future of a person. Thank you for exposing the plans of the devil and giving me the authority to cancel his evil works in my life. Thank you that the devil is defeated and I rule and reign in Christ Jesus. You have given authority and power over the works of the devil. Jesus has given me the victory. I am more than a conqueror through Christ Jesus who strengthens me. I am seated in heavenly places in Christ Jesus in Jesus' name. Amen.

Practice Exercise
Use the authority in the name of Jesus against the enemy in your situation. Cancel out the specific plan that he is doing against you. You can also do this for your family. This gift also is required for deliverance. Ask the Holy Spirit what areas of your life you need to break through from the cycles in your life. Once you know, you can do deliverance to break them. You need to know the root of the problem to cut it off completely. You need the scriptures to maintain your deliverance.

Lesson 8: Word of Wisdom

There are many experiences where the Lord revealed strategies of the enemy and gave insights into what needed to be done. He provided many ideas, solutions, counsel, visions, and more to resolve problems. He can guide you even in handling a court case and you will win when the Lord is on your side. The Lord knows the outcome. The Lord is the Judge and Jesus is our Advocate. He knows all the steps involved. If you follow His instructions, you will find success. He can guide you every day on what you need to do. He can also tell you if the case gets adjourned or rescheduled. He can even reveal the actual date and incidents that will happen that day. He can tell you the objections you need to present for your court case. He can tell you what He knows about the advocate and opposing party. He will reveal to you every detail if you ask Him. Many do not have this gift to be so accurately detailed to know all this. Usually, people only know that the case will be won. Very select few people will know more details. You may have heard of some prophets that can tell people their address and names of people with such precision. They may be able to tell exact details of the person's situation or what is to happen to them. It's a rare anointing. That person is usually that is very close to the Lord. There is also the gift of the panoramic that one servant of the Lord has been given. He can see the whole life of a person from beginning to possibly the end.

The word of wisdom is God's guidance for your situation. He will let you know the solutions and steps to deal with it. Prophets were used in the Bible to reveal the wisdom of God to the king and Israel.

Today, we have the body of Christ speaking God's word to us by the Holy Spirit. He gives us the counsel. The Lord can reveal the strategies, thoughts, and ideas He has concerning the situation. He will tell you what you need and how to deal with it. He will give you success to overcome it. If you are dealing with court cases, He will give you exact detailed information for each matter. He can tell you the objections, evidence you need, who you need to talk to, which advocate trusting or if you need one, the outcome in the court, reminders, understanding into the situation, thoughts about how the opposition will handle their part, their response and conversations, evidence and objections that they have, and the judge's decision. He can reveal also what happens after you have received the court outcome. He can tell you who to trust and which evil spirits are in operation among the people and what they represent and how you can fight and destroy them. He will show you also what He will do in your life when things are settled. When you are innocent, the Lord will avenge you and give you victory over your enemies. He will punish your accusers.

For the LORD gives wisdom; from his mouth come knowledge and understanding. (Proverbs 2:6)

Prayer
Father, thank you for the word of wisdom to counsel your people on what to do. Help me to speak the solution to the matter for the person to come out of their situation in Jesus' name. Thank you that I am walking in the solution that you have given for my life. That all crooked paths be made straight. I am established in Jesus' name. Amen.

Practice Exercise
Set a time to come before the Lord. Present the situation of concern to Him. Ask the Lord for the solution. Ask the Lord for His plan and speak it over your situation to be established in the name of Jesus. Believe that God's plan is done in your life. See yourself walking in God's plan. Apply what the Lord reveals to you. Then you will see the results. He may tell you what the final result for your situation will be.

Lesson 9: Prophetic Dreams

Joseph was given a dream twice that he would rule over his brothers and even the moon and the sun bowed to him. He didn't know the meaning of the dream until the Lord gave him the gift of interpretation. He was young and was unwise to share with his brothers. The Lord reveals future events in symbols. We need to understand what it means. Some dreams are warnings that we need to pay attention to and may require immediate action. They may be about urgent incidents like accidents that are about to happen. Joseph was warned in a dream to take Mary and Jesus to Egypt to escape King Herod. The Lord protects us from danger. Holy Spirit will reveal to us the interprestation of the dream. We must ask him for that. He allows us to intercede and change the situation by establishing His plan. We should ask Him what His plan is and pray for that to happen. You need to pay attention to all the details that you receive from the Lord to get the full understanding. Each individual or setting is symbolic. Plead the blood of Jesus before you sleep. You can ask the Lord to give you prophetic dreams.

My best friend receives a lot of dreams from the Lord that are prophetic. She shared one dream about 9/11 event before it happened. The Lord has also given me dreams about what He is going to do. He revealed in details places and people. He can show you your future life partner or a divine idea. He will give you precise details that you can write, draw, or record out what you saw in the dream. You will remember it. These dreams can change your future. The divine ideas are worth at least 2 million. The ideas are to help others. There is a requirement to return the tithe to the Lord out of the finances that we receive for the idea. It is ideal that your copyright and patent the idea that the Lord gives and know who to sell the idea to. The wrong people will steal your idea and you will lose out on the financial benefits too. The purpose is to bring glory back to the Lord and finance His kingdom. The Lord can bring you to places even without you physically leaving too. He can transport your spiritual man to certain places to meet certain people. You will fulfill a divine purpose each time you have these kinds of encounters. The Lord can give you encounters with Him too.

The Lord gave me a dream about the enemy's plans. He can make this known to us. He will give the strategies against it. There are dreams where the Lord showed that He would grant me opportunities and promotions. There is also a dream where I was talking to my prayer partner and then a portal opened up where he reached out his arms and I put my hands under them to receive an impartation. The Lord granted joy out of that. There are people that see their house that the Lord promised them or receive an idea. The vision of Microsoft's Windows came from a dream and was given by the Lord. The owner of the company has not acknowledged that God gave him this idea. Some people received songs through dreams, poems, dances, businesses, or names. A number of them don't realize God gave them these. The ideas we receive through dreams, visions, and listening to God are rich. When people hear about it, they will invest a lot of money into them. The ideas can resolve problems that man cannot accomplish on their own. It can benefit billions of people.

Joseph dreamed that his sheaf stood upright and all his brother's sheaves bowed before his. The sun and the moon also bowed to his sheaf.

Then he remembered his dreams about them and said to them, "You are spies! You have come to see where our land is unprotected."
(Genesis 42:9)

God gives dreams of heaven, hell, people, and other places. Dreams can be changed, but visions can't be. The repeating dreams will stop once we know the message and deal with the source of the problem. We might have dreams that come from ourselves or the devil. Nightmares come from the devil. Jesus has given us authority to cancel them and pray for God's plan to replace it. We must ask God what His plan is in order to replace the enemy's plan. I had a dream where I was looking into a file cabinet with all the names that began with the letter A. When I asked for the interpretation; the message given is that it will position me to me among those who are at the top. The Lord will grant me honour and promote me. Many times, I dreamed about my family in different settings. Sometimes the dreams are good and other times it is revealing an issue that God wants removed. I had dreams about going to school, too. I found it strange since I have completed my education already, but it symbolically meant God is training me. Sometimes, God may want you to go get further education to accomplish His calling. Symbols mean different things to people. If you dream about driving a vehicle, that vehicle represents ministry. The speed it travels shows how fast you are progressing. You can ask God to grant you prophetic dreams and ask for the interpretation. He will grant it to you. The Bible has other examples of dreams. Joseph interpreted the chief butler, chief baker, and Pharaoh's dreams. The Holy Spirit has the gift of interpretation. He also gives us the gift to dream prophetically. We also must obey the instructions given to us after we understand the dream and the solution. Sometimes we will dream of people that we never met. They may represent somebody in our life or somebody we will meet.

He has given people dreams about Jesus coming to visit people in the late night. Jesus can also give you a vision in the late night. Some ministers and believers said that the best time to receive from the Lord is at 3a.m. Pray and seek Him and He will answer you.

Prayer

Father, thank you for all the examples in the Bible about dreams. Cover me with your blood and cleanse my mind, body, and emotions. You give your beloved sweet sleep. My heart desires to receive prophetic dreams so that I can know the future. Give me an understanding of the dreams and the ability to remember them when I wake up. Prepare my heart and equip me for your purpose. Bring the right people into my life. Protect me from receiving any other dreams that don't come from you. Guide me to walk in the direction for them to be fulfilled in my life in Jesus' name. Amen.

Practice Exercise

Write down the dreams that the Lord gives you. Ask the Holy Spirit to reveal to you what the symbols mean. Ask for directions on what to do and start to walk out of His instructions that He gives. Some prophetic dreams are for a later time, so you need to pray into them.

Lesson 10: Equipping and Purity

Lesson 10: Equipping and Purity
In the New Testament, the prophet is assigned to equip the saints. He is to also give corrections and warnings. The office gift of the prophet is different than the prophetic gift. It is an appointed position that the Lord assigns to specific individuals. The training takes years for the person's character to be shaped. They can't have pride in their heart. They are very accurate in their prophetic gift. Not everyone recognizes a prophet, especially one that is in training but has not been ordained and appointed as one by the church. The Lord can ordain His people directly without using people to do it. He can do this through a vision. He lay hands directly to ordain and gives the authority too. These servants of God are usually humble and don't promote themselves. The Lord will promote them before the people. He will cause those He chooses to recognize their assigned position. Often the pure ones are those that people don't know. They serve without being recognized for their title.

Holy Spirit wants a clean vessel that He can abide in to serve the Lord and reveal about the Lord. He will rest on us. The more yielded you are the more the Lord can use you mightily. Our goal should be to please Him. Let the anointing flow through you to minister to others. Always keep yourself spiritually clean. Repentance should be done daily and plead the blood of Jesus over you. It's wise to also claim Psalm 91 and Ephesians 6:10-18 for protection at the start of your day. We need to be ready for resistance. "For we wrestle not against flesh and blood, but principalities, against powers, against the rulers of the darkness of this world, against spiritual wickedness in high places." (Ephesians 6:12) We often forget that we are battling the spirits and not people. The enemy uses people to work against us. Stand firm on the Word of God in all circumstances that you face.

The Lord will speak to you everything that you need to know about a person as you ask Him. Maintain your walk by having sufficient time with Him daily. The deeper relationship is with the Lord the more you will be able to live out of His presence daily even when you work you will be able to hear His voice speaking to you. The more you seek Him the more you will develop spiritually in the anointing and gifts. Your spiritual senses are sharpened. A prophet or prophetess must go through much training and transformation. They also endure many hardships in life to form their character. The Lord has to prune each of us so that we will be purified and be able to glorify Him fully through our lives. People need to see Christ demonstrated through our lives. Worship, prayer, bible reading, and spending with the Lord alone every day and in addition to spending time with a prayer partner regularly. It will maintain accountability. Those who are pure in heart will see the Lord. We should become more like Christ every day. Allow the Holy Spirit to develop your character.

You may also see angels. Everyone has their angels. We have at least two angels and I found out last year that I have three angels and the third one is named Joy because the Lord knows that I need it. The angels of the Lord will minister with you and they can tell you things. They are assigned to aid us in the purpose of God, so we need to use our authority to send them forth to work on our behalf.

Prayer
Father, bring the right people to train me to increase in the prophetic gift. Increase the prophetic flow in my life. Develop my character every day. Purify my walk with you and that I will stay in your presence. Give me a clean conscience and an upright heart to remain in you daily. Teach me how to send my angels to go forth and do your work in Jesus' name. Amen.

Practice Exercise
Make time to learn more about the prophetic and to practice it. Set time alone to ask the Lord to show you your angels and to guide you have to command them to do God's work. Whatever is the calling that God has for your life you can ask the angels to assist in getting that work done. They can lead you to opportunities that you need to get to. They will guide you when you need to go there and who to meet with. The angels are your servants and not to be worshipped.

Lesson 11: Intercession and Warfare

Intercession is about praying for others' needs and their situation. It means to stand on behalf of them or stand in the gap. They can also be assigned tasks involving spiritual mapping and certain prayer assignments for the Lord. They need to be properly trained for prayer and often spend time alone with the Lord. The intercessors can become very close with the Lord in their relationship. They are often in God's presence regularly and they can pray for several hours a day. The Lord reveals to them what is on His mind and heart. He gives them a heart of compassion for others. There are different kinds of intercessors and they all can be prophetic. Abraham, Moses, King David, Daniel, Nehemiah, Ezra, Queen Esther, Anna the prophetess, are some intercessors though some of them are also anointed for more. You can read into their life to discover also about their life of prayer for others. Joshua and Jesus' mother Mary, Simeon from Jesus childhood, and Lazarus' sister Mary are also examples of people who sought the Lord closely and also were regularly in the presence of the Lord.

The Lord will train you in intercession. Spiritual warriors are assigned to do the warfare, but intercessors take on the attacks of the enemy, which they need to plead the blood of Jesus over themselves daily and always stayed protected. They can experience difficulties and the Lord also enables them to feel what the other feels or thinks. He can reveal things to them about the person's situation through different methods.

I urge, then, first of all, that petitions, prayers, intercession and thanksgiving be made for all people. for kings and all those in authority, that we may live peaceful and quiet lives in all godliness and holiness. (1 Timothy 2:1-2)

It is an intercessor's responsibility to pray for everyone that God assigns in your life as well as for those in authority. Your family, relatives, friends, church leaders and church, prayer group if they are not in the church, boss, manager, supervisors, colleagues, teachers, neighbours, the bank staff that handles your finances, charities you volunteer at, govern ment leaders and workers, postman, newspaper delivery person, etc. Pray also for the neighbourhood, city, nation, and you can pray for the world.

An intercessor can be trained to do spiritual warfare. Intercessors can experience backlash from the enemy if they haven't protected themselves. They should declare Psalm 91, the Armour of God, and the blood of Jesus to cover them daily. An apostolic and prophetic leader also has an anointing for intercession. It is how they become great leaders for the Lord. They must first be great people of prayer and faith.

I was also previously trained in some aspect of spiritual warfare but didn't know about the warfare in defeating the demon spirits. There are those God has chosen and equipped to be spiritual warriors for Him.

Their job is to fight against the demon spirits. They don't just use the scriptures, but they make war in the spirit with spiritual weapons or supernatural strength that the Lord has given them to fight. Most people are afraid to fight back or are only take the authority to bind and lose. The enemy can return to attack again if we open the door, so unless they are defeated they can't come back. The Lord showed in visions what spirits need to be dealt with and what they represent. Then it is our job to defeat them completely. The Lord will give us the vision of our victory over them. The best spiritual warfare is when we pray by the Holy Spirit. It is the most effective way to fight. We need to have faith that the Lord has enabled us to destroy the evil spirits and they can't return. They will fear us. Jesus did this ministry though it is not mentioned in the Bible. He has the authority and power to destroy the evil spirits completely. He taught us in the Bible to cast them out, but we need to make sure that they don't return.

Most people are taught to use the scripture for spiritual warfare or to pray in tongues. The Lord may assign them to do other things even declaration and worship. There are those constantly praying in the spirit and

There is warfare that you pray in tongues against the evil spirits to destroy them. It is done with another believer that shares the same mind, heart, and spirit as you. They may be more mature and their ages could be very several years apart. They must be more experienced and knowledgeable in this area. The devils will listen to anyone who has the authority and calling to defeat them. Believers can take authority over them but not everyone is called to destroy them. The Lord will equip those who have this calling. This also requires revelation, wisdom, knowledge, discernment, vision, and the ability to sense them. You would need to know how to strategically fight against them. Ideally, believers must use scriptures. Jesus also used scripture against the devil. He called him by name and commanded them to leave. He knew its function too. Their destiny is hellfire. Evil spirits will usually respond when questioned.

There are cases where the evil spirit may reveal what they have done against you or somebody else. They are able to inflict and steal, kill, and destroy where there is a legal right. They may be the cause of certain problems that you experience. He can also block you from getting the results God promised you or delay them.

Many are the afflictions of the righteous, But the Lord delivers him out of them all. (Psalm 34:19)

We are afflicted in every way, but not crushed; perplexed, but not despairing; persecuted, but not forsaken; struck down, but not destroyed; always carrying about in the body the dying of Jesus, so that the life of Jesus also may be manifested in our body.read more.
(2 Corinthians 4:8-11)

And He was casting out a demon, and it was mute; when the demon had gone out, the mute man spoke; and the crowds were amazed. (Luke 11:14) rebuking the enemy. Healing and deliverance prayers can also be consid ered as part of warfare, but it does have their ministry. It is usually on the condition of the individual to maintain their walk with the Lord to keep the evil spirits from coming back again. There are so many kinds of deliverance prayers that believers can declare to come out of generational curses, bondages, personal sins, iniquities, and transgressions. Soul ties have to be cut and it can become a very tedious and lengthy process sometimes. They must plead the blood of Jesus and have the cross involved in it too.

Forgiveness is also required and they may also request believers to do lots of scripture-based declarations and tell them to repeat until they are fully persuaded and that their mind has been transformed.

There are repetitive sins that people find themselves not able to come out of too. The truth truly sets us free indeed. The other is symptoms that keep coming back when we receive healing from sickness or disease. Often, they keep praying prayers over thinking that they are not free. We need to realize and ask the Lord how to deal with each matter. He knows the best way for us to be set free. We might need those strategies that are being taught by different ministers, but if a believer keeps thinking they need deliverance it becomes a problem. They will need to renew their mind to align with the Bible.

You must be properly prepared before you do spiritual warfare. Unless you have been assigned and anointed to do the spiritual warfare, you must plead the blood of Jesus and use the scriptures and pray in tongues. Make sure that you have declared Psalm 91 and put on the armor of God from Ephesians 6:10-18 because you will be faced with severe opposition from the enemy. When you know who you are in Christ and have been anointed for the warfare, the evil spirits cannot stand against you. A royal priesthood and a special people will not be defeated. You will have the authority to destroy them from the operation.

There is a warfare that you pray in tongues against the evil spirits to destroy them. It is done with another believer that shares the same mind, heart, and spirit as you. They may be more mature and age could be very several years apart. They must be more experienced and knowledgeable in this area. The devils will listen to anyone who has the authority and calling to defeat them. Believers can take authority over them but not everyone is called to destroy them. The Lord will equip those who have this calling. This also requires revelation, wisdom, knowledge, discernment, vision, and ability to sense them. You would need to know how to strategically fight against them. Ideally believers must use scriptures. Jesus also used scripture against the devil. He called him by name and commanded them to leave. He knew its function too. Their destiny is hellfire. The evil spirits will usually respond when questioned.

Prayer
Father, equip and teach me in intercession and warfare. Holy Spirit pray through me. Give me the words to pray. Thank you for the gift of intercession and warfare. Impart of patience that is needed to wage the good warfare that is required. Protect me as I intercede on behalf of others. No weapon formed against me will prosper and every tongue that rises against me will be condemned for this is the heritage of the servants of the Lord and He is my righteousness. I am more than a conqueror through Christ Jesus who strengthens me. Thank you for the strength to fight spiritual warfare. Open my spiritual senses to see and defeat my enemies. Like Jesus, I can take authority over the evil spirits working against me and my loved ones in Jesus' name. Amen.

Practice Exercise
Make time to pray with the Lord for others. Spend time to pray specifically for those on your heart and that the Lord leads you to pray for. You also need time to do the warfare. You need to take the prayers seriously. If the Lord has not given you the anointing to do spiritual warfare, you must limit yourself to using the scriptures. This is your warfare and praying in tongues. Do not use any other methods as there are going to be consequences. The enemy knows when you don't know your authority and identity in Christ. If you do it on your strength, you will be defeated.

Lesson 12: Authority

There is another level of prayer, which involves taking authority in the name of Jesus. The Lord told his disciples that he had given them authority over all principalities and powers. Those of us in Christ also have been given the same authority. He wants us to use it to change circumstances. This is the life of victory in Christ. The enemy doesn't want you to know your authority or to use it. He will bring people into your life that will become a hindrance to you. You will need to discern what spirits are working against you and to ask the Lord to reveal it to you. Then take your authority and use it. You need this also when you speak prophetically because you may be doing deliverance on a person when releasing a word to them. We have been given the power to bless others, which cancels curses and brings them to a new level to receive from the Lord. It will advance their life. The words spoken have power over the person's life to effectively change their life destiny. Take authority over every word that comes against you.

Jesus could have used His authority to heal Lazarus before he died. He knew everything before it happened yet He chose to wait until Lazarus was buried to use His authority to raise the dead.

The prophetic is also given to save a person from danger. The Lord can use you to take the authority to deliver the person from their current situation to a situation that is yet to happen. He will give you the message to warn them and unction to take the authority to cancel it with the person's permission. There is a time when somebody mentioned a sickness. The word was for somebody that I know. I had to check with the person that I know to find out if they had that and they didn't know or heard anything from the doctor. My pastor told me to reject it and don't accept it. I took authority over it so that it cannot come to that person and text the person to let them know. The person agreed with my prayer. We still need to be praying and aware. Some people may tell you a negative word. That is when we must test it and take the authority to cancel it. There may be a requirement that we have to check our walk with the Lord to see if we have fallen into sin. If we have, then we must repent and obey the Lord.

Casting down imaginations, and every high thing that exalteth itself against the knowledge of God, and bringing into captivity every thought to the obedience of Christ; (2 Corinthians 10:5)

No weapon that is formed against thee shall prosper; and every tongue that shall rise against thee in judgment thou shalt condemn. This is the heritage of the servants of the Lord, and their righteousness is of me, saith the Lord. (Isaiah 54:17)

Submit yourselves therefore to God. Resist the devil, and he will flee from you. (James 4:7)

Behold, I have given you authority to tread on serpents and scorpions, and overall the power of the enemy and nothing shall hurt you.
(Luke 10:19)

And Jesus came and said to them, "All authority in heaven and on earth has been given to me. (Matthew 28:18)

And these signs will accompany those who believe: in my name, they will cast out demons; they will speak in new tongues; they will pick up serpents with their hands; and if they drink any deadly poison, it will not hurt them; they will lay their hands on the sick, and they will recover."
(Mark 16:17-18)

Truly, I say to you, whatever you bind on earth shall be bound in heaven, and whatever you loose on earth shall be loosed in heaven.
(Matthew 18:18)

"Truly, truly, I say to you, whoever believes in me will also do the works that I do, and greater works than these will he do because I am going to the Father. (John 14:12)

His divine power has granted to us all things that pertain to life and god-liness, through the knowledge of him who called us to his glory and ex-cellence, (2 Peter 1:3)

Creation is anxiously waiting for the sons of God to rise and take their authority on the earth to rule and have dominion. When you speak your prophetic destiny, you advance the kingdom of God and you also bring yourself into the purpose of God. As you keep praying in tongues, you speed your spiritual growth and advance your destiny to happen. You also cause the plans of the enemy to be destroyed. You have more access to what the Lord has promised to you a lot sooner and easier. The authority is given to you also can be used to release others into their destiny. It can also speed their growth. You can command circumstances to line up with favor according to God's plan for your life or their life. When you use the authority, you break the cycles that have been a blockage. You connect divine connections and you cut off wrong connections. You have access to the resources that were hidden, stolen, and withheld. The Lord has given us all authority, so be confident to use that authority. You have control over whatever the enemy does in your life. Some changes will take time to manifest, but the changes will happen. You can take authority over the people over the evil that they are doing. You can take authority over things and cleanse them from impurity.

One sister blessed more than her food but also blessed the people who produced it and every person involved in the process. She blessed even those who provided the utilities we use and the products that we purchase. We can also take authority over the evil that is behind people that are against us. This also applies to taking authority over the leaders in their decisions too.

You can take authority over the decisions made in the courtroom and government as the Lord leads you. Many decisions are made with or without divine intervention. It's a recent revelation that came to mind. Many of the evil plans going on should be stopped when the leaders and believers take authority over them and call forth God's divine plan and judgment against them.

The authority in the name of Jesus also has the power to control the weather. We can change the weather before it happens just by taking authority over it and speaking that it will be a sunny day. We can command

Remember anyone can prophesy:
Even on My bondslaves, both men and women,
I will in those days pour forth of My Spirit
And they shall prophesy. (Acts 2:18)

We need to be motivated by love:
Love never fails; but if there are gifts of prophecy, they will be done away; if there are tongues, they will cease; if there is knowledge, it will be done away. (1 Corinthians 13:8)

Prayer
Father, teach how-to walk-in authority every day and to take authority over the enemy's works. I cancel the works of the enemy operating against me in my home, family, church, job, business, and life in Jesus' name. I release the plan of God to become established in my life in Jesus' name. Protect everything that belongs to me including my family, job, and business in Jesus' name. In Jesus' name, my life is blessed, prosperous, and successful for the Lord. That I will have everything that the Lord has promised and become a blessing to others. I will fulfill the works God has assigned for my life. I will continue to walk upright with a humble heart and in purity. That I will glorify the Lord all the days of my life in Jesus' name. Amen.

Practice Exercise
Take time to use the authority that Christ has given to you in areas of your life that have been affected by the enemy. You will see breakthroughs in those areas. You can do this for your relationships, your neighborhood, city, country, and more. Take authority over every situation that needs a breakthrough. Then you will see victory in that area.

the weather to change when it is not favourable at the moment we are living in.

And he arose, and rebuked the wind, and said unto the sea, Peace, be still. And the wind ceased, and there was a great calm. (Mark 4:39)

We can take authority over the enemy's plan operating against us in our home, job, business, family, church, pets, relatives, friends, colleagues, neighbourhood, city, nation, government, world, etc. You can also speak over what you own. You can put a restraint that the enemy cannot pass that barrier that you create with your confession or the word of God. Decrees are also effective. You can change the results of the economy or even a government leader can be changed but it must align with God's plan. We may not always see the results we expect. The motive in how it is prayed affects these prayers. You will be accountable for what you pray for others. Everyone has a different level of authority that is related to the particular ministry God assigned for them.

You can command a change into your future when you take authority in the name of Jesus Christ. Praying in tongues is also another way that your life will come into its destiny and can speed up the fulfillment of God's plan in your life. It also destroys the works of the devil in your life and other people's lives. You should ask the Lord for the interpretation to understand what you are praying for.

The authority in the name of Jesus also has the power to control the weather. We can change the weather before it happens just by taking authority over it and speaking that it will be a sunny day. We can command the weather to change when it is not favourable at the moment we are living in.

And he arose, and rebuked the wind, and said unto the sea, Peace, be still. And the wind ceased, and there was a great calm. (Mark 4:39)

Lesson 13: Preparing for ministry

Practice the prophetic gift everyday first on yourself. Look at the mirror and speak over yourself. Faith confession and declare scriptures over yourself. You will notice yourself transform after time and your confident will increase. Confirm with the scriptures once you have received prophetic words. You can begin with journaling to listen to God and journal or record the prophetic words that you receive when you are alone. You need to test them before you minister to others. Make sure you have a mentor that is gifted in the prophetic and can discern the prophetic words and one that will train you further in the gift. They should be able to recognize if you have the seer's anointing or called to become a prophet for the Lord. They should encourage and be able to equip you into that calling. Then they will guide you on how to walk with the Lord to enter into your ministry and give you the platform to operate in the gift. If the Lord has spoken to them, they will also know when to send you out to minister to others outside of the church. Prophets are sent out when they are appointed and set apart for the prophet's ministry. Then they will not remain in the local church as often but travel to other churches or places to minister.

I started in a group that was training believers interested in the gift of prophecy. We would pray in tongues every time before we released a prophetic word. There were always those more experienced and already walking in the gift among us. They would test the words given to ensure that it is from the Lord. They also had prophetic prebysters assigned by the church leadership that gave prophetic words every week. Whoever the Lord led them to minister, that person was called forward and the church would record the word and give the copy to the receiver to listen to again and keep. It was the receiver's responsibility to walk in obedience to the Lord and to pray over the prophetic words given until they are fulfilled in their lives. They must know whether it is from the Lord. You will experience confirmation from your spirit man too.

Neglect not the gift that is in thee, which was given thee by prophecy, with the laying on of the hands of the presbytery. (1 Timothy 4:14)

The Lord will ask you to connect to the person you need to minister to. If they agree for you to release it, then take the opportunity and trust the Lord for the delivery of the word. You may sense a strong conviction to release the word to the person. If the person is unwilling, you take the prophetic word before the Lord. Pray for the person. You can have it recorded. Pray for the Lord to touch their heart that they will be open to receive it. You will know when to release the word to them. The Lord may give you another opportunity but you can still pray for them especially if it is an urgent message. Life or death scenarios require you to urgently intercede for the person. You need to make sure that the person who received the word responds back to you. You will know based on their response if it is a confirmation or needs to prayed further.

He has decided who will work with you to fulfill His plan. You will know when you meet the person. Holy Spirit will reveal that to you. Sometimes the individual(s) may not know that they are assigned to work with you. They will need to grow in their relationship with the Lord and be trained in the gifts and in the knowledge of the Word of God. They need to have a regular prayer life too. They will need to seek God to get confirmation. You need to pray for them regularly.

Prayer
Father, thank you for anointing me for ministry. Holy Spirit lead my steps to minister to the people that you want me to release the prophetic words too. Protect my mind, body, emotions, and heart. Cover me in the blood of Jesus Christ. Remind me of scriptures and minister through me the message you want released to each person. Open their hearts to receive your words and see them fulfilled in their lives. I pray for your presence to be with me. Give me accuracy in hearing and receiving from you in Jesus name. Amen.

Practice Exercise
Ask the Holy Spirit to show you who to minister the prophetic word. He will tell you or show you the person. Take action to connect with the person and ask them first. Let them know that the Lord has given you a word for them. Release the word and ask them to respond.

Salvation Prayer

God, I know that I have sinned against you. Forgive me for the wrong that I have done. I believe that Jesus Christ died on the cross for me and that He was became rose from the grave. That I can have His eternal life. Come into my heart to be my Lord and Savior. I choose to turn away from my sins and to follow you. Lead me to walk with you. Keep me safe and teach me your ways. I cancel every plan of the enemy against my life. I renounce every covenant that I have made. I take authority in Jesus' name to close every open door in my life. Holy Spirit fill me now in Jesus' name. Amen.

Baptism in the Holy Spirit

Jesus you are the one that fills me with Your Holy Spirit. Come Holy Spirit and come into my life and fill me to overflow with Your presence. Come with your fire too. Thank you for the gift of tongues and your anointing in Jesus' name. Amen.

Open your mouth and let the words come out that God gives you. It will be words that you don't know what they mean. God can give you the meaning when you ask Him. Keep giving God your mouth to speak it out. You need to let Him talk through you every day to grow this gift. He will also take you closer to God and you will know more about Jesus and have power from God to do great things and know things.

Prayer

Father God, thank you for the gift of prophecy. Activate and anoint me to fully operate in this gift that I can minister to others who need a word from you. Thank you for the Holy Spirit which is the giver of the gifts. Empower me to walk in it daily and to receive dreams and visions. Grant me also the interpretation. I pray that your name will be glorified through my life in Jesus' name. Amen.

Message from the Author

The Lord inspired me to write this book on Flowing in the Prophetic. The prophetic is one of the strongest and most accurate that the Lord has given. Holy Spirit welcomes us to have a close relationship with Him just as much as with Father God and Jesus Christ. Each one has a different function and personality. Holy Spirit is a gentleman and will not force you to do anything but will remind you about the Word of God. We can easily ignore Him without realizing it. Often when we are busy or occupied with other thoughts, we will not realize that He is speaking to us. I found that when I minister to others I hear the Lord more clearly. He will respond immediately and provide the necessary details that He wants to speak. He will activate various gifts based on people's needs. The gifts are not for our own benefit but for others. We are called to build up the body of Christ and to minister to those who don't know the Lord. We are to use the gifts to minister to them and lead them to Christ. This book also is good for a teaching series and will allow believers to have a coach to guide them into practicing the prophetic gift and receiving a prophetic word. This gift needs to be practiced and nurtured to maturity. The flow will become natural and increase over time. You will become more precise and detailed. There was one person the Lord revealed that they would meet a businesswoman for a meeting and sign a deal for a business venture. The Lord also granted him a car and he was wearing a business suit. In another case, the Lord showed that land is going to be for sale and the amount it will be sold at. There was also a scene of some businesswoman carrying a clipboard and another businessman drafting up a contract. These are prophetic and yet to be confirmed by the individual that received the word. You need to be anointed also to get this kind of prophetic insight and revelation. You can email me if you are interested in the prophetic. You can check out my website towards the end of the book and check my other books.

Testimony

In my personal experience, I received names, dates, numbers, places, visions, dreams, scriptures, detailed instructions, solutions, ideas, poems, songs, lyrics, motives, and the source of the person's problems and situations. The Lord also revealed the attitude and characteristics of people. When I spent time alone with the Lord, He would also give me prophetic songs. They are songs about the Lord's bridal relationship with the Church.

There is a time that I was told about a company that I would work for and the Lord revealed that the office has three rows of tables and described how they were laid out and that there are 2-3 people mainly working in that part of the office. It is an open-concept workstation area. The desks have brown surfaces. I would get the job for the interview that I went for. They will hire me. I had to ask a friend about how to find work and I applied to job posting on Indeed. There were two companies that were supposed to interview, but it turned out only one had successfully happened.

The day of the interview; they had snow piled up, and the transit was delayed. They did not clear the snow on the sidewalks because there was a snowstorm recently, a day or two before. I was late for the interview, but the staff proceeded with the interview. I had to explain my lateness to them, too. They were understanding and told me I have potential and that they would speak to the owner and decide. They decided they wanted to hire me and give me an opportunity to learn. They said that we can try for two weeks and see if I enjoy working there. I received a confirmation email that same afternoon that they hired me. I agreed to start work on Monday. It was Wednesday when I had the interview. I was still expecting the other company, but they never contacted me. I took this job and worked there until I took on another job that I wanted more. There are lessons, skills, and experiences that I had to gain through this job. I had to learn to schedule and plan my time wisely. They limited me on time before and after work. In a vision, I was told that I should do payroll for my career. I started taking an accounting course in March.

I had to take the basic Accounting before I could study the Payroll courses. It was available online so I could study from home. It worked out to my advantage because of my schedule. I had to learn on my own and complete the exams and exercises on time. The Lord helped me to succeed even when there were difficult topics.

I got a better job instead and could quit the job I was doing. The current job has given me the opportunity to study part-time on payroll. I also prophesied that I would get into the job that I wanted more. It happened. I had to wait for a time for it to happen. Somebody also prophesied over me. He said that I would get a better job around Resurrection Day, but the prayer is they will give the job earlier and it happened a few weeks earlier. The Lord granted me favour among my manager and colleagues. I need to learn from my colleagues and get along with everyone. This will grant me other opportunities, including learning how to become a manager. They gave me the opportunity to take part in the training committee. By faith, I trusted the Lord for the finances to pay for the payroll courses while I still had debt to pay off. The Lord had dealt with the previous manager at another office to make him quit the job. I also had time to write my books and improve on books that I have previously published.

I continued to have more visions when I spent time in prayer. He also granted additional spiritual gifts such as interpretation of tongues, the ability to smell a scent with my spiritual nose. There was one other gift which was briefly introduced but also forgotten. I had an interesting imparting of joy dream too. I saw a portal open up with two hands of my friend reaching out to me and he laid them on top of my hands. I saw the bright light. Many of the visions I received are prophetic.

I proceeded with the first payroll course after the accounting. It overlapped with the end of my accounting course. I had to study for both courses at the same time for about a month. I was successful in completing the first payroll course and continued onto the second, which they only allowed to be taken one course at a time.

Index

OTHER PRODUCTS

The Bridal Collection
Knowing God
How to Hear God's Voice
New Life in Jesus
Loving Israel
God's Gifts
Meeting God
Word Power
Fruit of the Spirit
The Tabernacle
Bride for Jesus
A Life of Prayer
Live Free
Who am I in Jesus
Walk in Love
God's Favor
Man of God
Woman of God
How to Use Money
God's Wisdom
Fasting
See Jerusalem and Bethany
First Fruit Offering
Pentecost
Feast of Trumpets
Day of Atonement
Feast of Tabernacles
Counting the Omer
Festival of Lights
Glory, Presence, and Holy Spirit
Live in God's Presence

31 Day Devotional
Biblical Puzzle Book Vol 1
Biblical Puzzle Book Vol 2
Biblical Puzzle Book Vol 3
Biblical Puzzle Book Vol 4
Biblical Puzzle Book Vol 5
Bible Puzzles for Young Children Book 1
Bible Puzzles for Young Children Book 2
Bible Puzzles for Young Children Book 3
Biblical Puzzles for Children Book 1
Biblical Puzzles for Children Book 2
Biblical Puzzles for Children Book 3
Smokey the Cat

Teaching Series & Guides
How to Hear God's Voice Teaching Guide
Knowing God, Jesus, and Holy Spirit
Relationship with God, Jesus,
Holy Spirit Guide

And much more!

Please check Chelsea's website for links to other books and products found onAmazon, Barnes and Noble, and Kobo. Please leave a review to help the author to write more books.

https://chelseak532002550.wordpress.com

YouTube channel:
https://www.youtube.com/channel/UCOvw9wUmkE08Akeq2z3TQVA

Coaching Products

Teaching Series Packages to train you to equip you for God's purpose!

Check the website for details:
https://chelseak532002550.wordpress.com

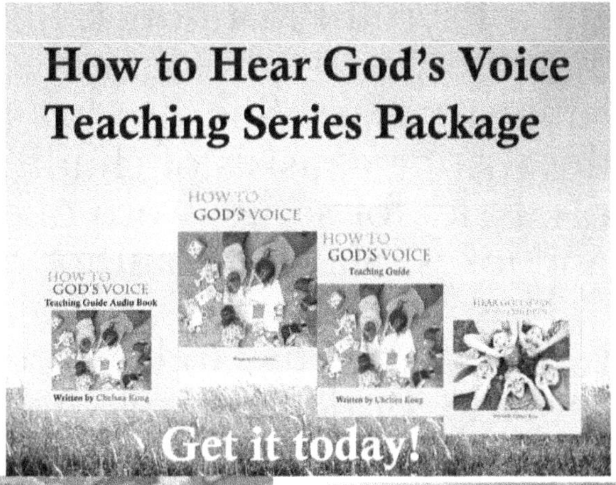

Learn How to Hear God's Voice
Knowing Him
Build a Relationship with Him

Each package includes lessons and
related books

Chelsea Kong Biography

She is a writer, creative arts and digital media artist, and skilled administrative professional. She graduated from Hotel and Restaurant Management, Digital Media Arts, Office Administration, and is studying to become a Payroll Practitioner. She also served in a variety of roles from audio visual, photography, to assisting on the worship team, and ministry team. She also has a passion for families being united. Her writing consists of children books, stories, bridal writing, poems, lyrics for songs, word of encouragement, blessings, prayers, and jokes. She is the author of the Bridal Collection, Knowing God, How to Hear God's Voice, New Life in Jesus, Loving Israel, God's Gifts, Meeting God, Word Power, Fruit of the Spirit, The Tabernacle, Bride for Jesus, A Life of Prayer, and etc. She also has her own Bible Puzzle books and other inspired products. These books teach children principles about faith and Christian life. She also has her own 31 days devotional, audiobook, teaching series on How to Hear God's Voice, Relationship series, and other inspired products. She is an organizer and tour guide for Favor Tour Ministries. Her podcast channel on self-development called Chelsea K on Anchor, Spotify, iTunes, and etc. Her podcasts can also be found on YouTube. She was interviewed on TheLadyTraceyShow on UnityLive Radio. She has an article published in the Readers Magnet and highly recommended by A Proud Christian blog.

www.ingramcontent.com/pod-product-compliance
Lightning Source LLC
Chambersburg PA
CBHW080333030726
47593CB00010B/2993